ROYAL
CAROUSELS

DONNA FREITAG

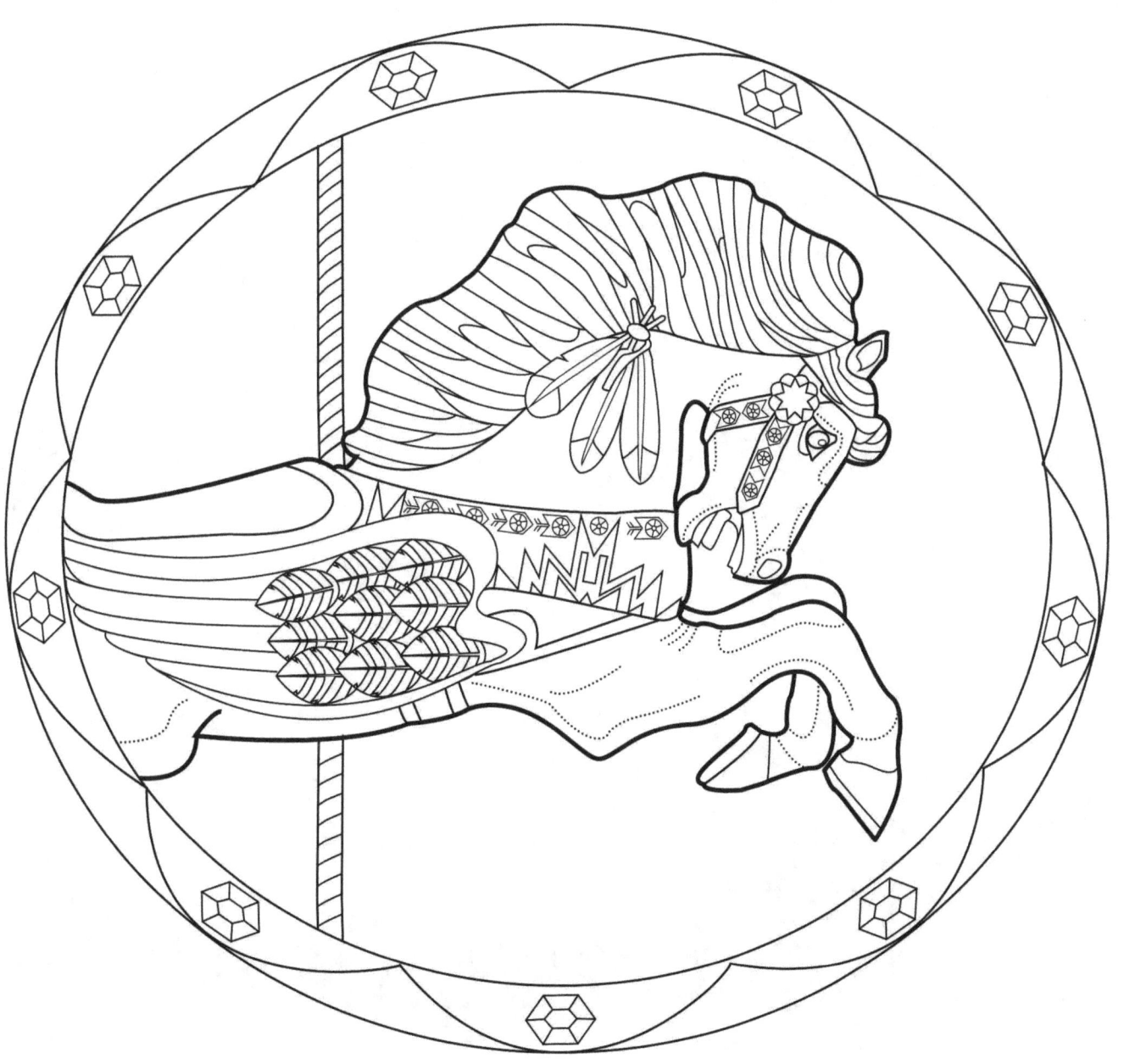

DONNAFREITAG.COM

How to color this book

Royal Carousels is a coloring book for adults. You'll enjoy hours of creative, relaxing, stress relieving fun as you color 25 all new space age designs. All are beautiful, new, original artwork never before seen in any collection.

Coloring Tips

Colored pencils are the most popular way to color. It's best to get a large set of at least 48 colors. Some of the best brands are Prismacolor and Staedtler.

In addition, you'll need an eraser and a good pencil sharpener. Also popular are markers. Warning: they tend to bleed through the page. So if you use them, place a sheet or thick paper underneath so the ink doesn't leak onto the picture below. Copic markers are a great brand.

Marker sets offer a smaller choice of colors than pencil sets. That's one reason why the pro colorists often use a combination of pencils, markers, gel pens and even crayons.

It all depends on the effects you want to produce.

Please post photos of your artwork on my Facebook page. I'd love to see what you've done!

Royal Carousel Horses and Animals, and the Famous People Who Rode Them.

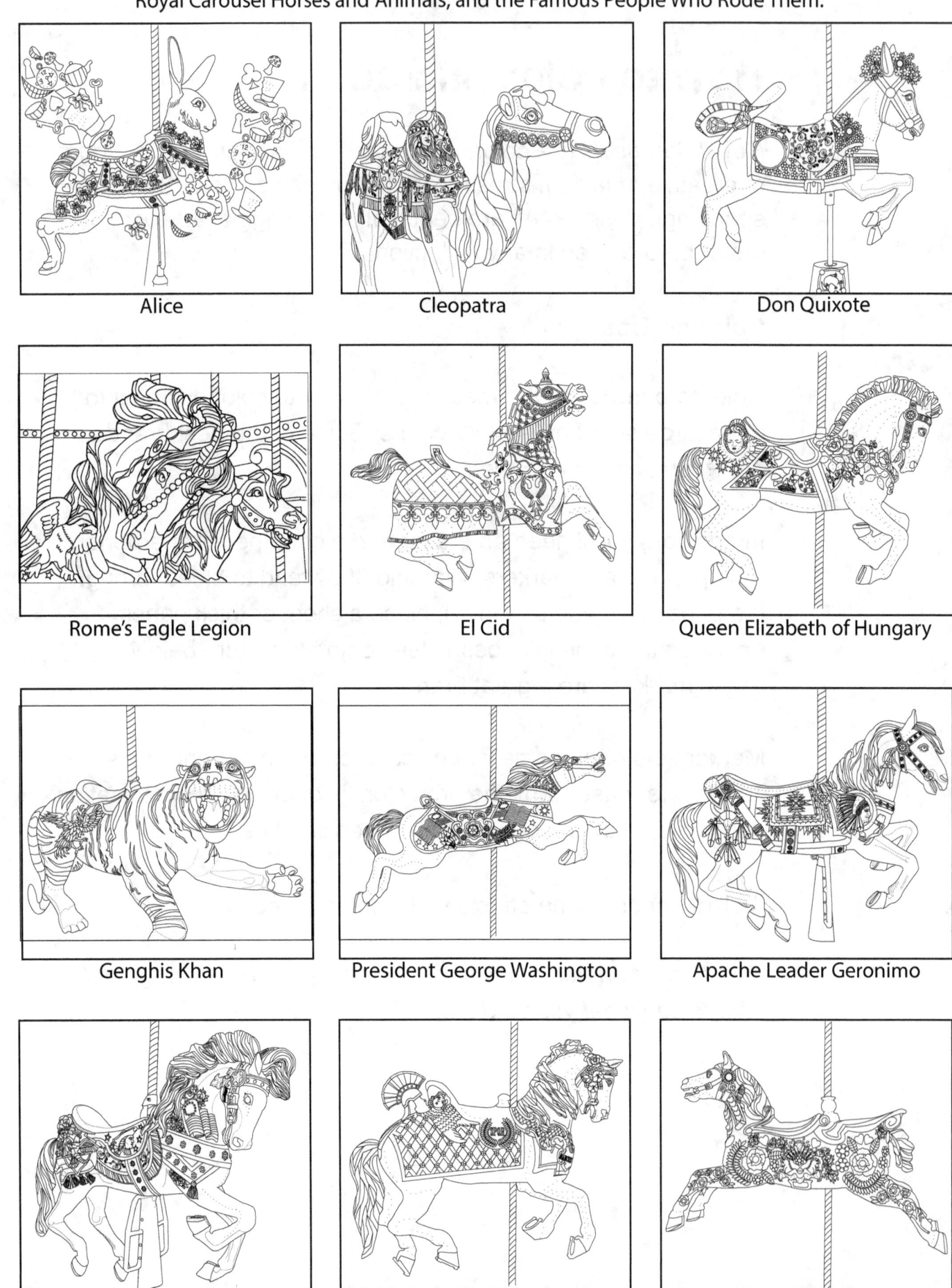

Alice

Cleopatra

Don Quixote

Rome's Eagle Legion

El Cid

Queen Elizabeth of Hungary

Genghis Khan

President George Washington

Apache Leader Geronimo

Paul Revere

Emperor Marcus Aurelius

Artist Henri Rousseau

Royal Carousel Horses and Animals, and the Famous People Who Rode Them.

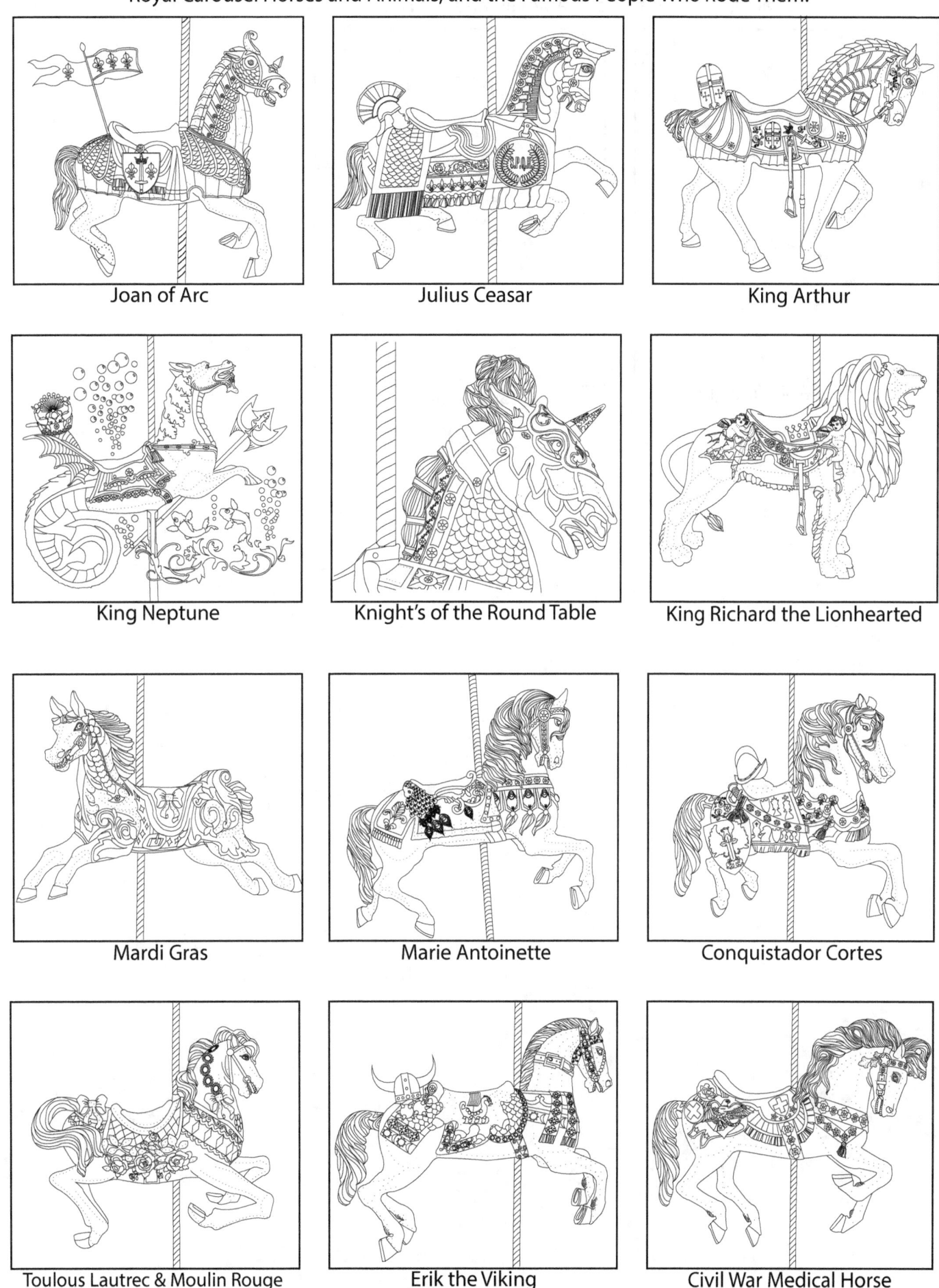

Joan of Arc

Julius Ceasar

King Arthur

King Neptune

Knight's of the Round Table

King Richard the Lionhearted

Mardi Gras

Marie Antoinette

Conquistador Cortes

Toulous Lautrec & Moulin Rouge

Erik the Viking

Civil War Medical Horse

Royal Carousel Horses and Animals, and the Famous People Who Rode Them.

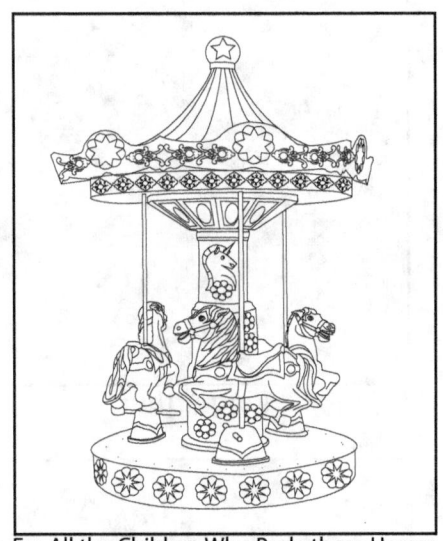

For All the Children Who Rode these Horses

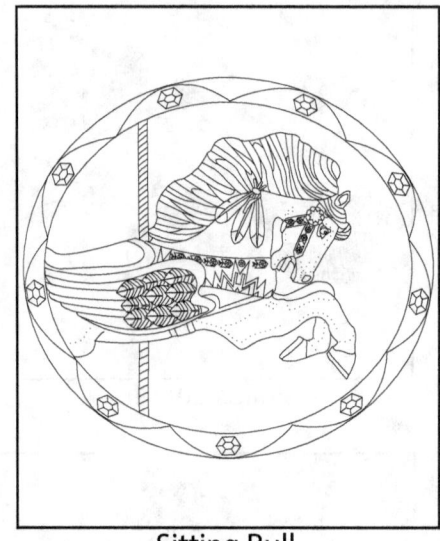

Sitting Bull

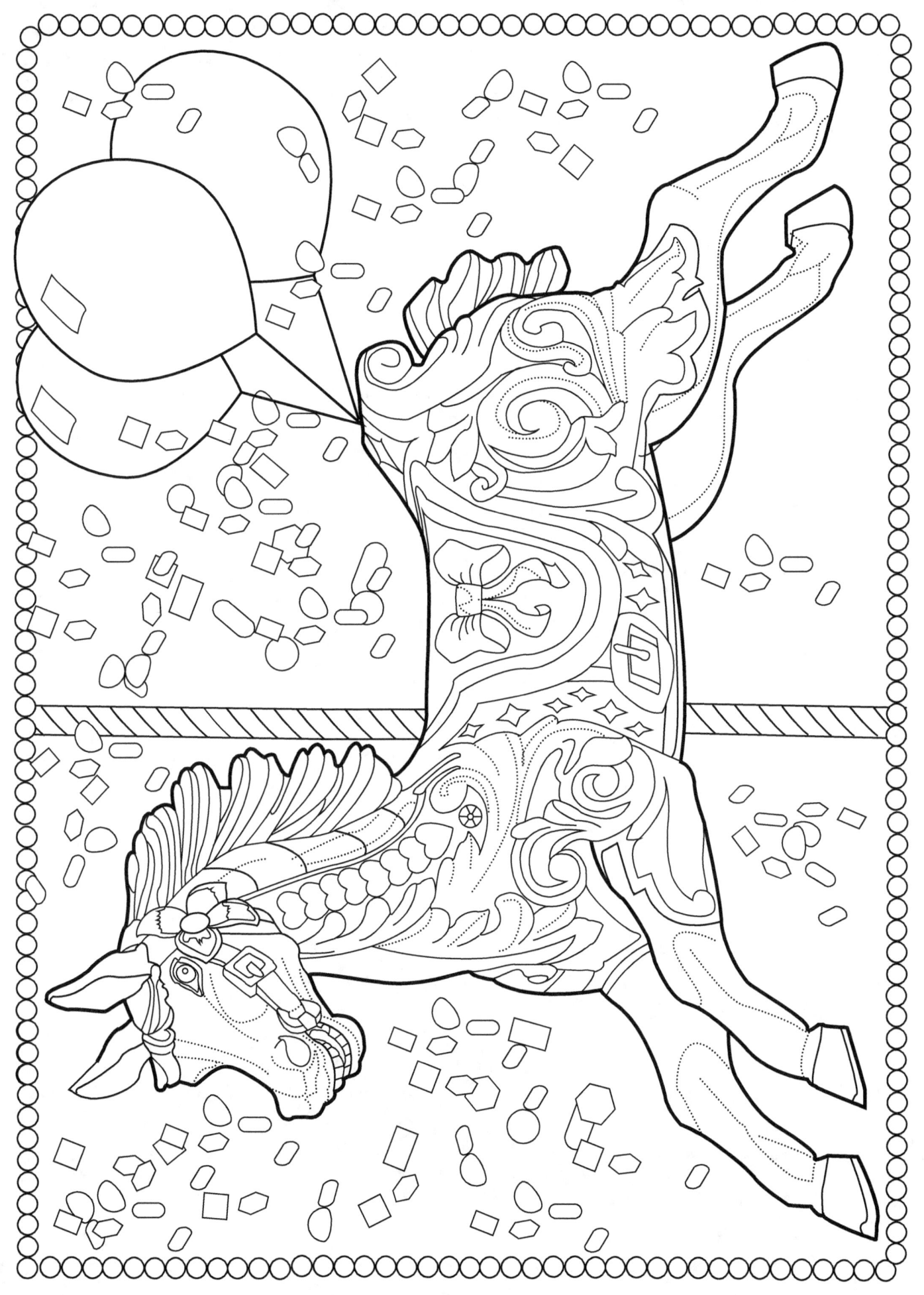

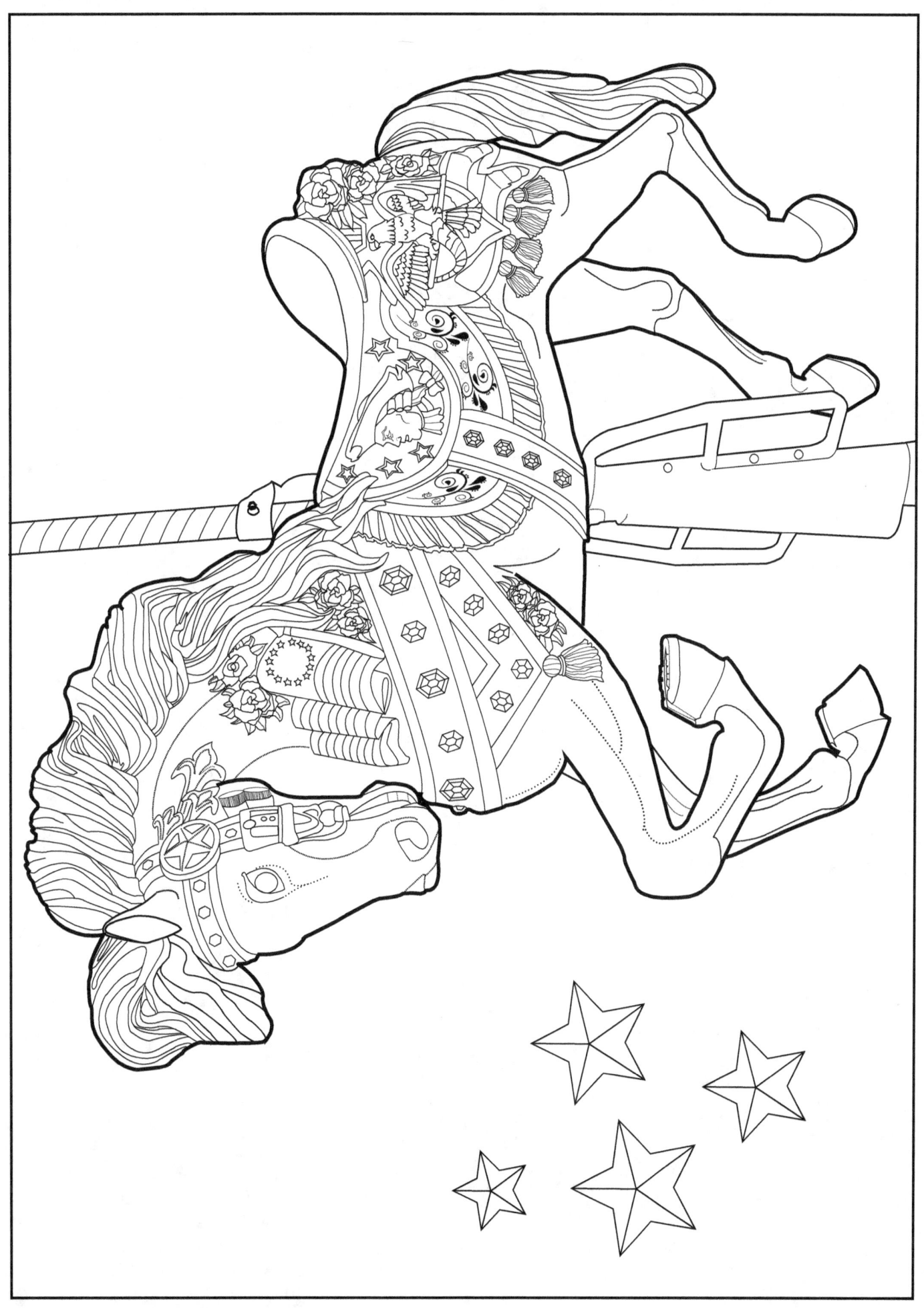

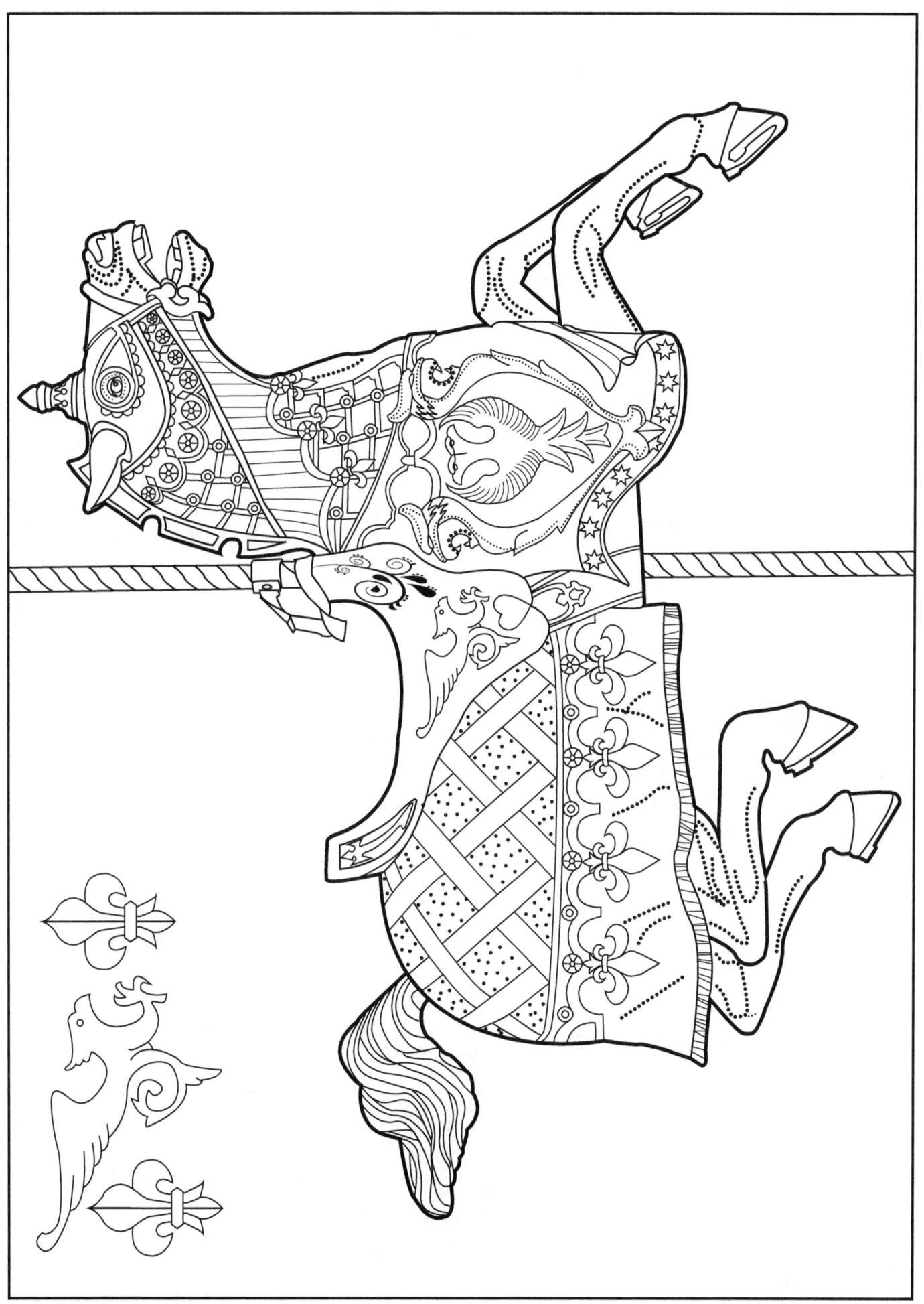

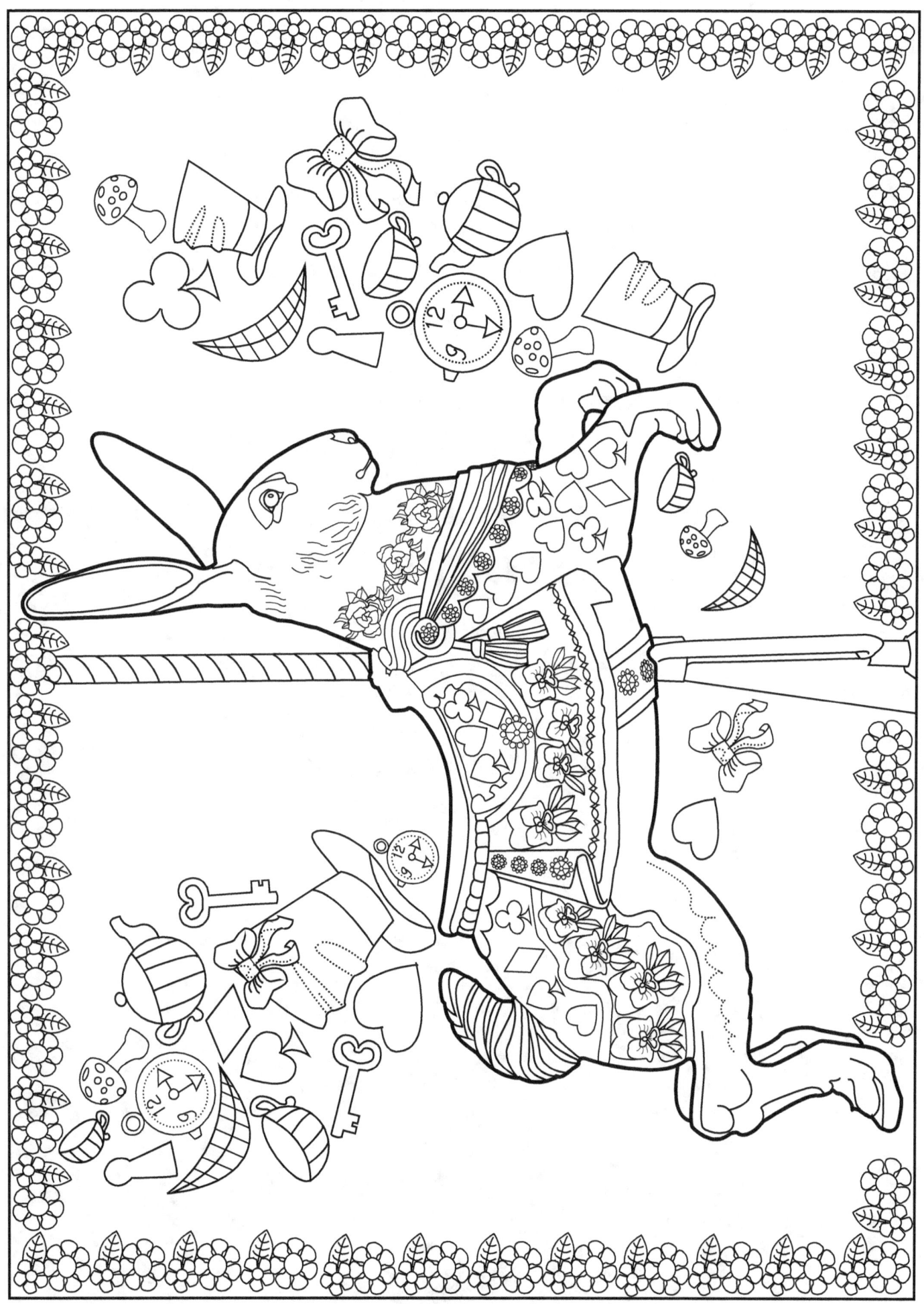

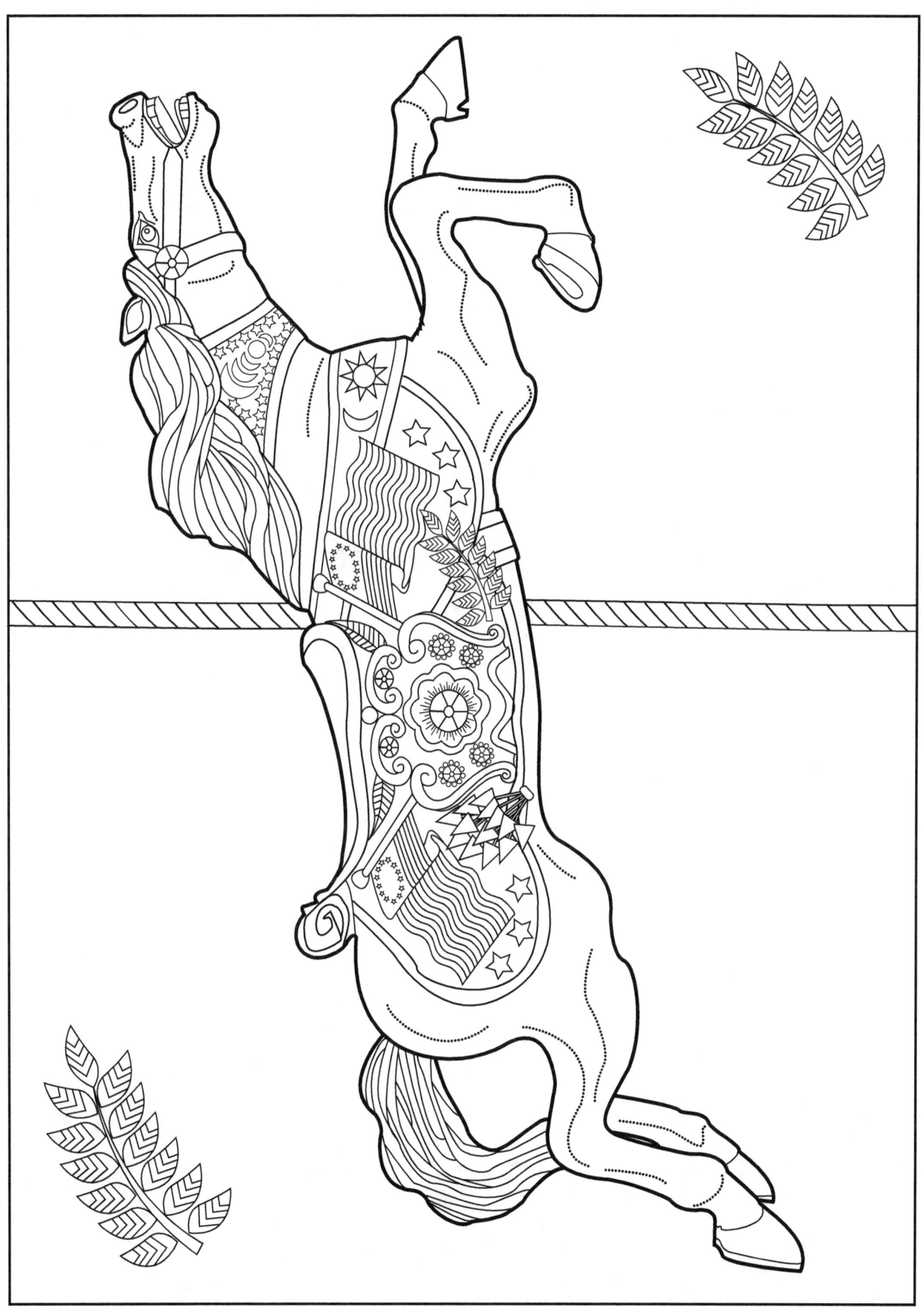

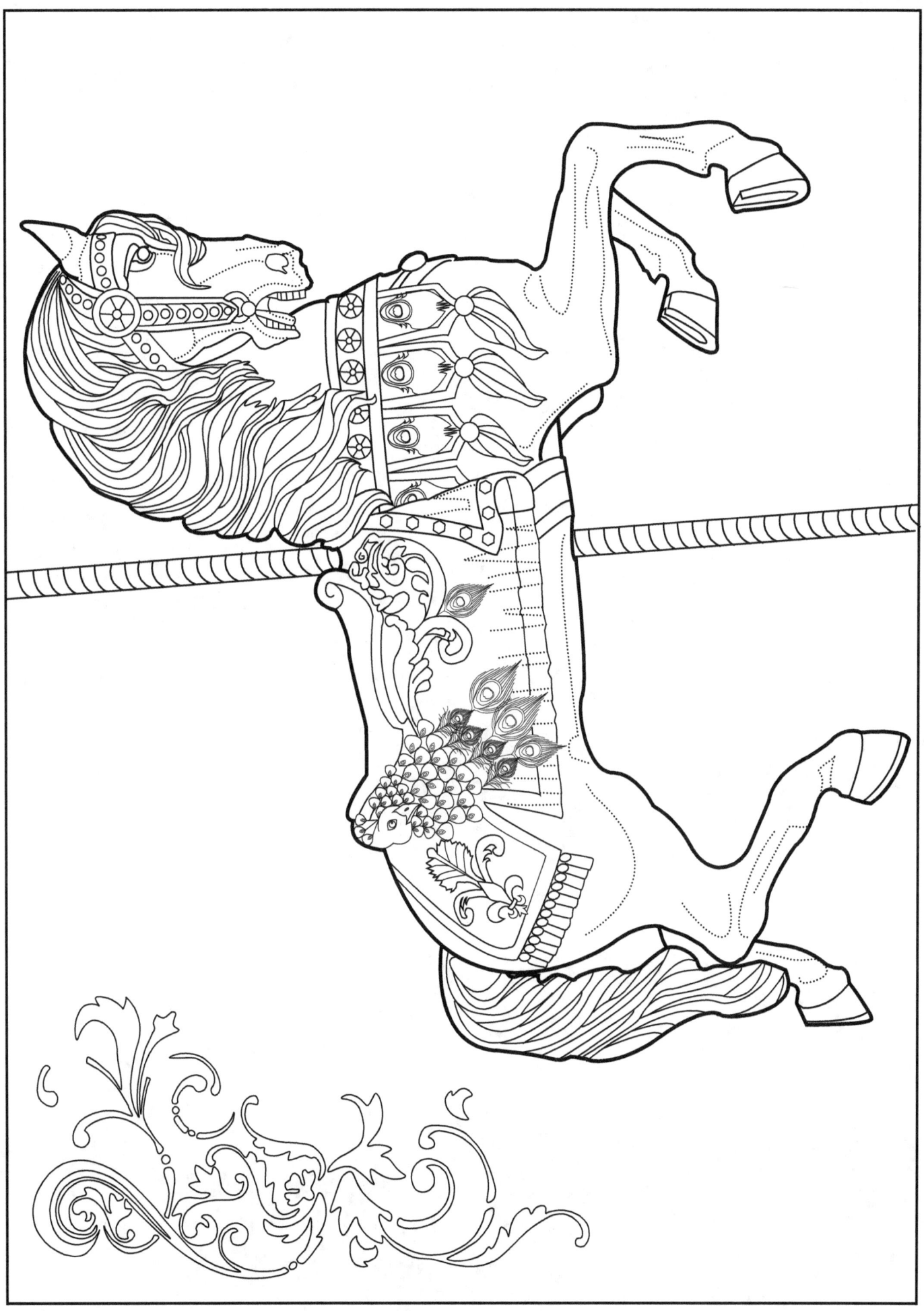

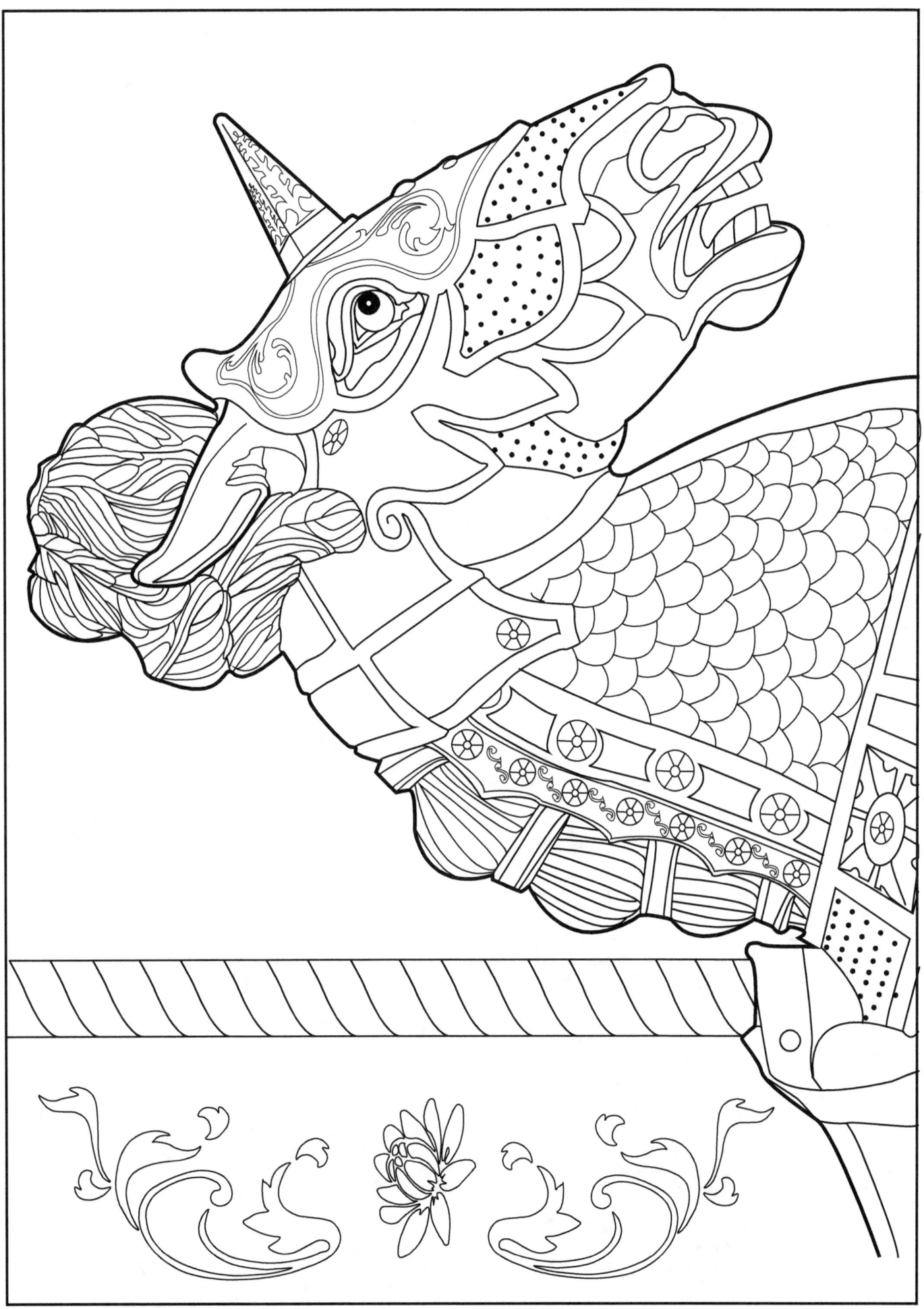

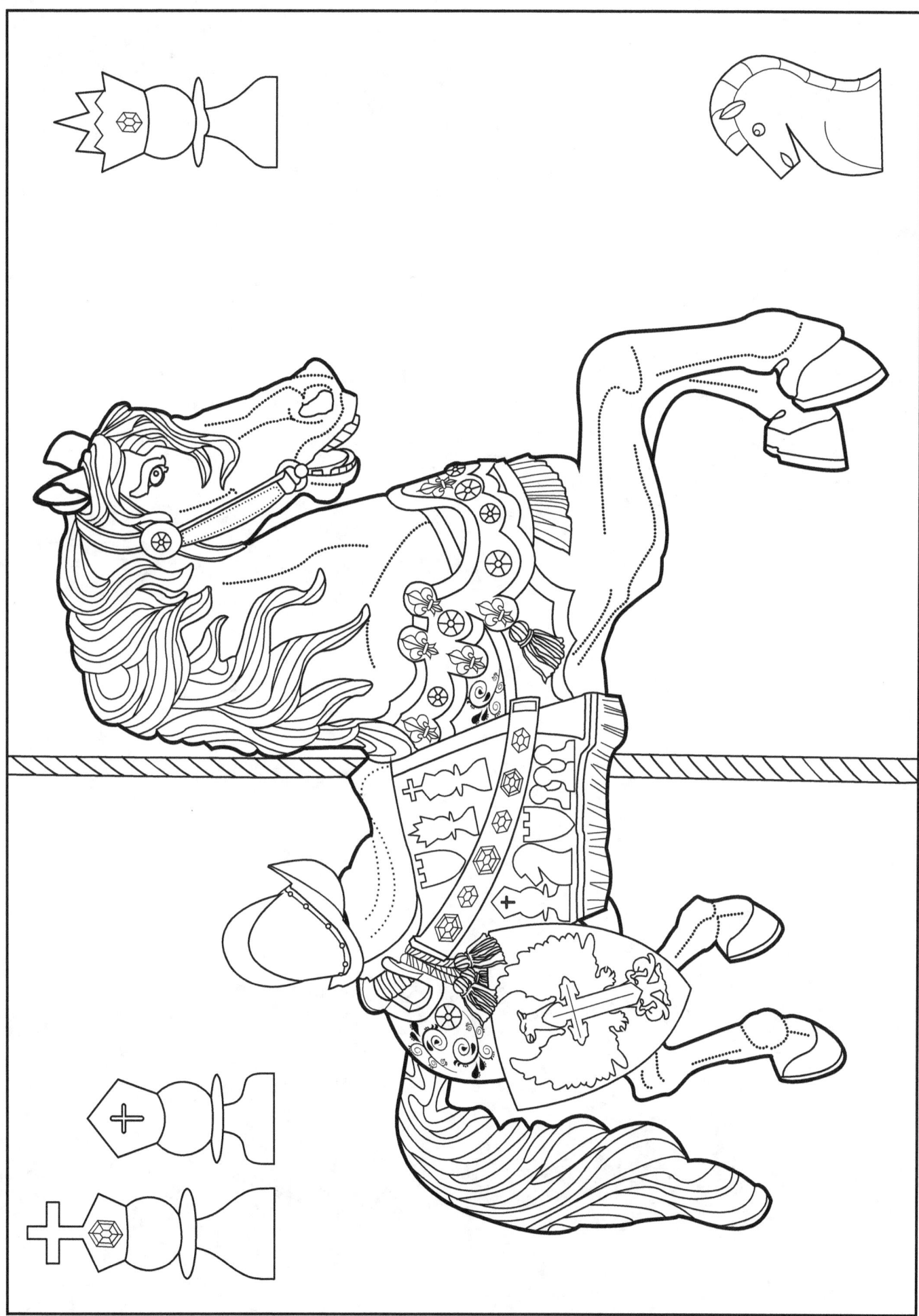

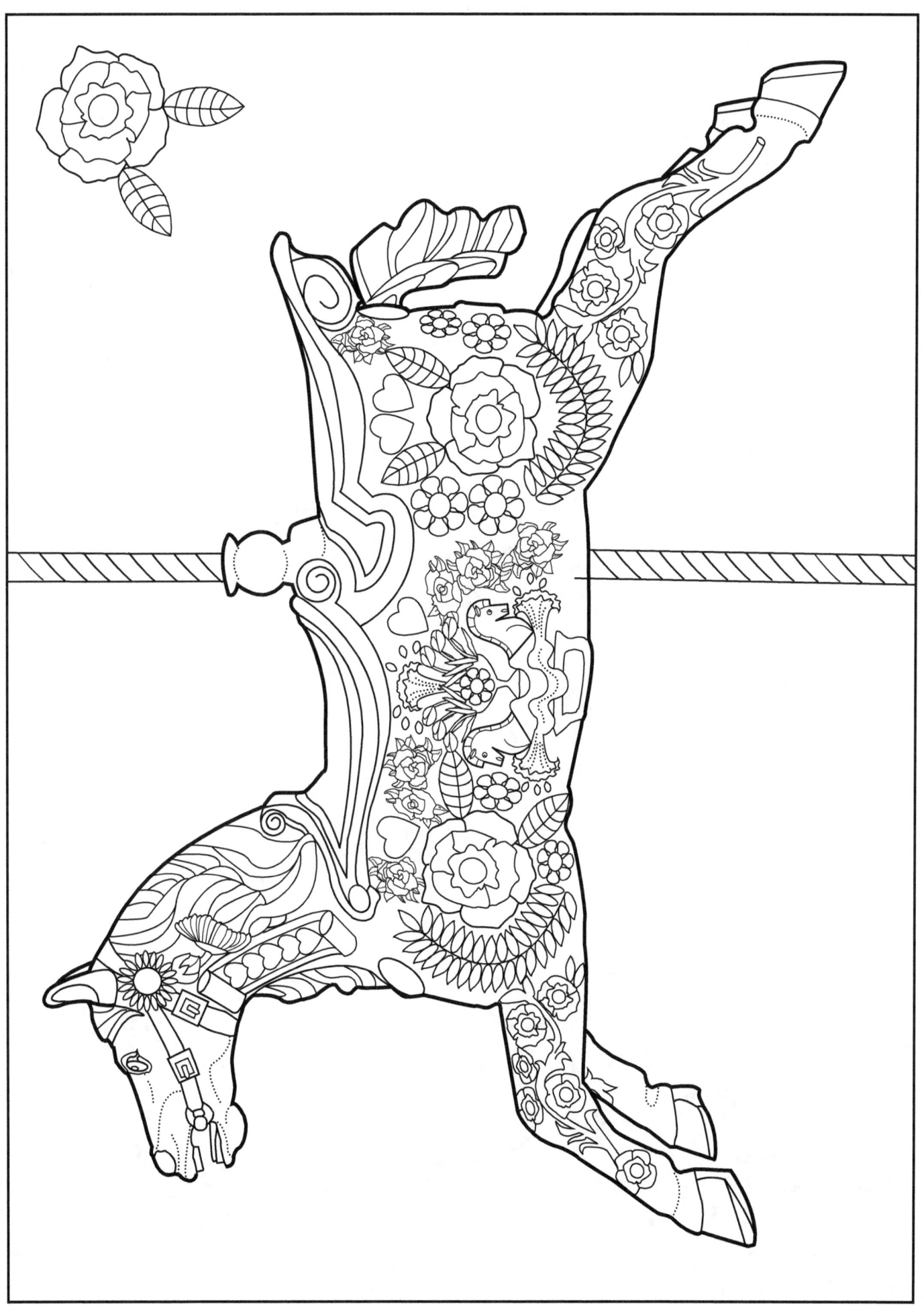

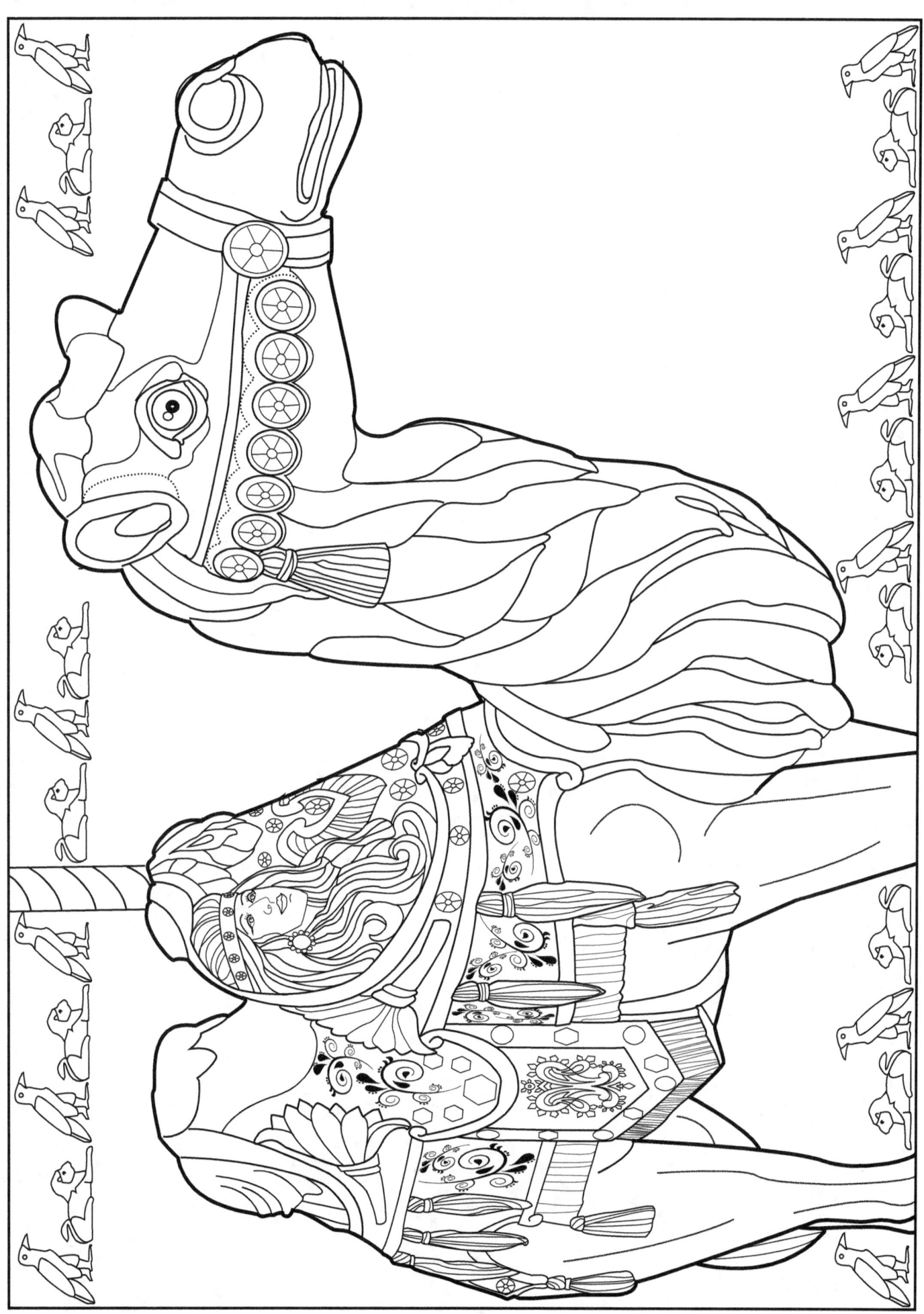

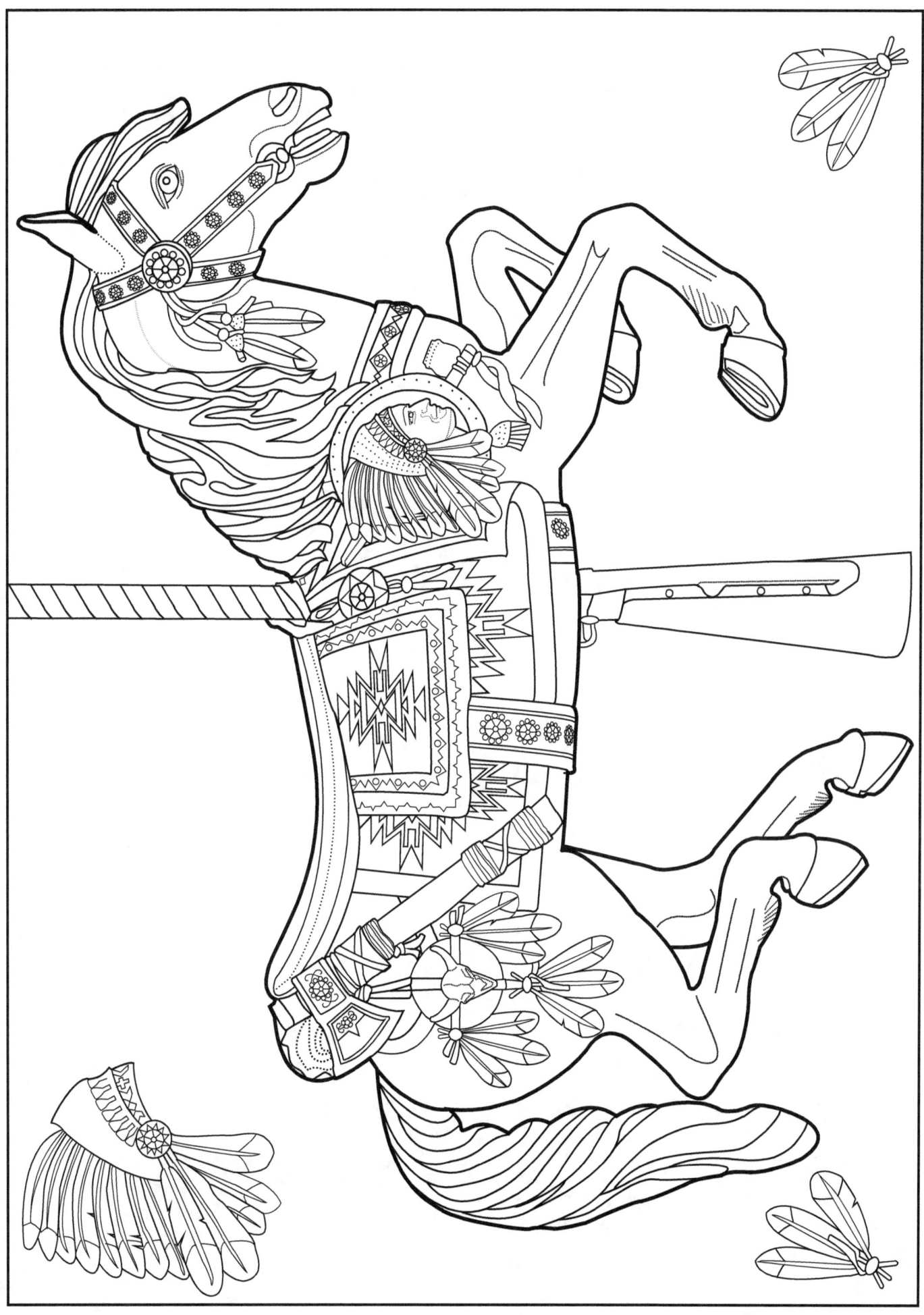

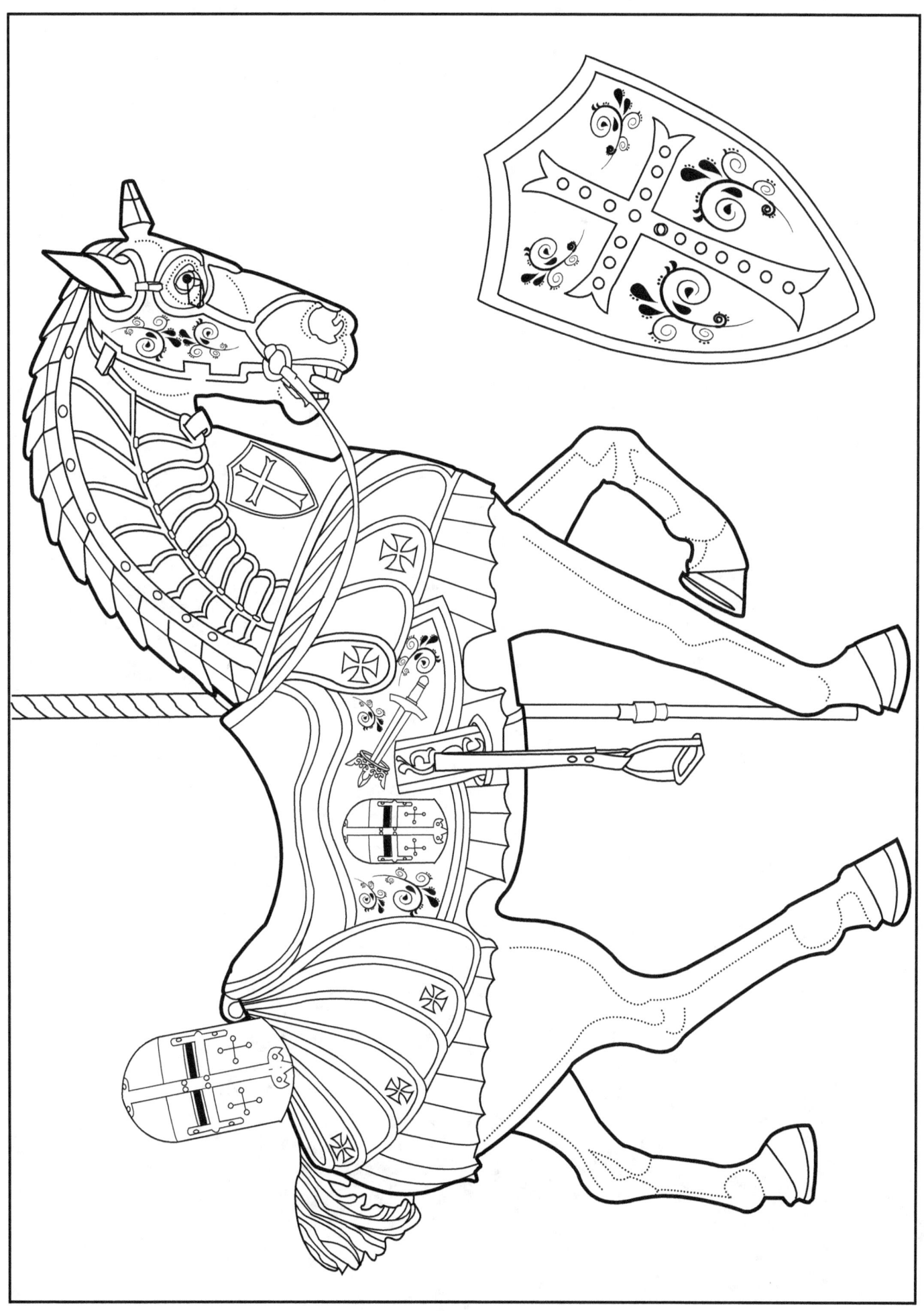

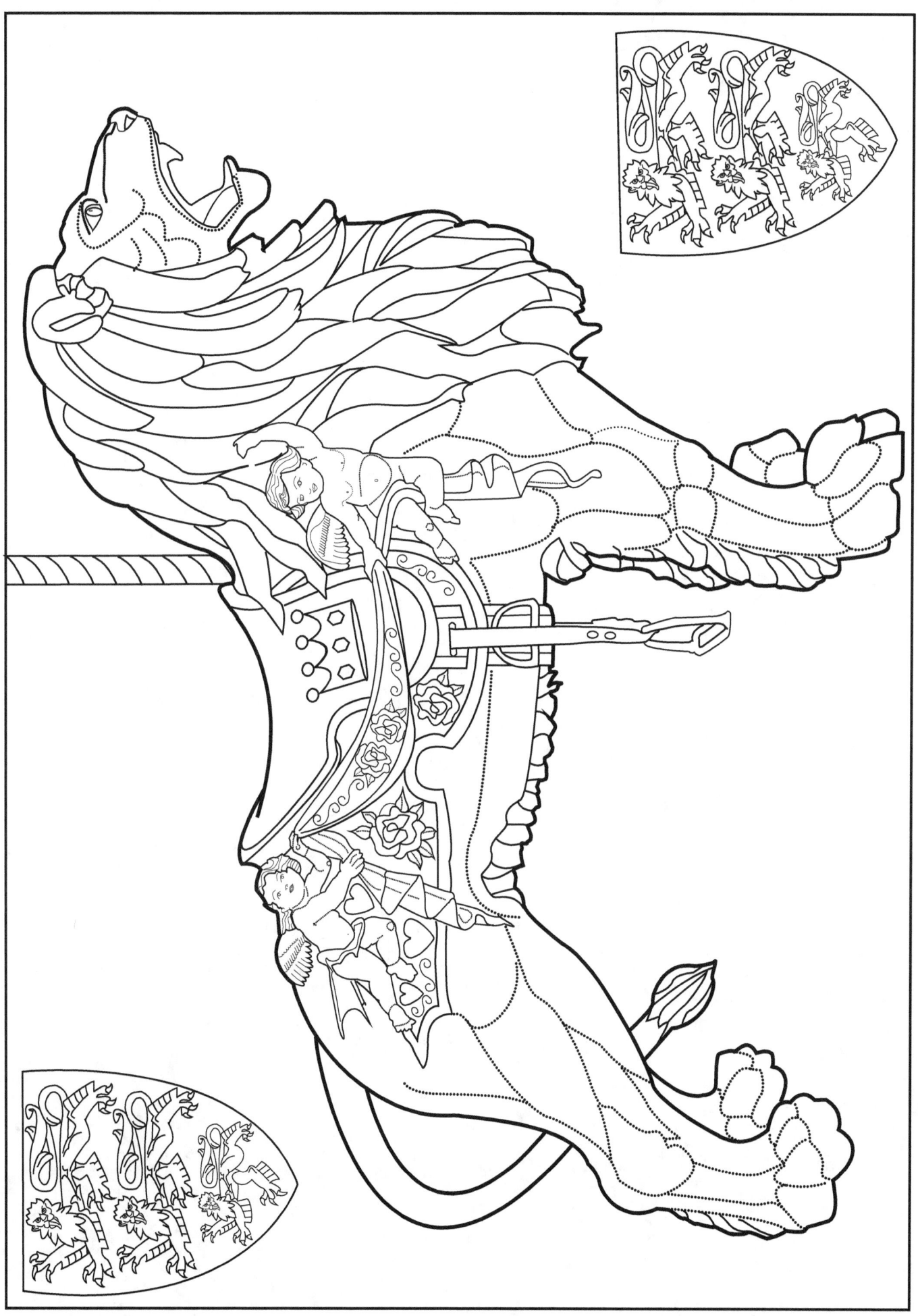

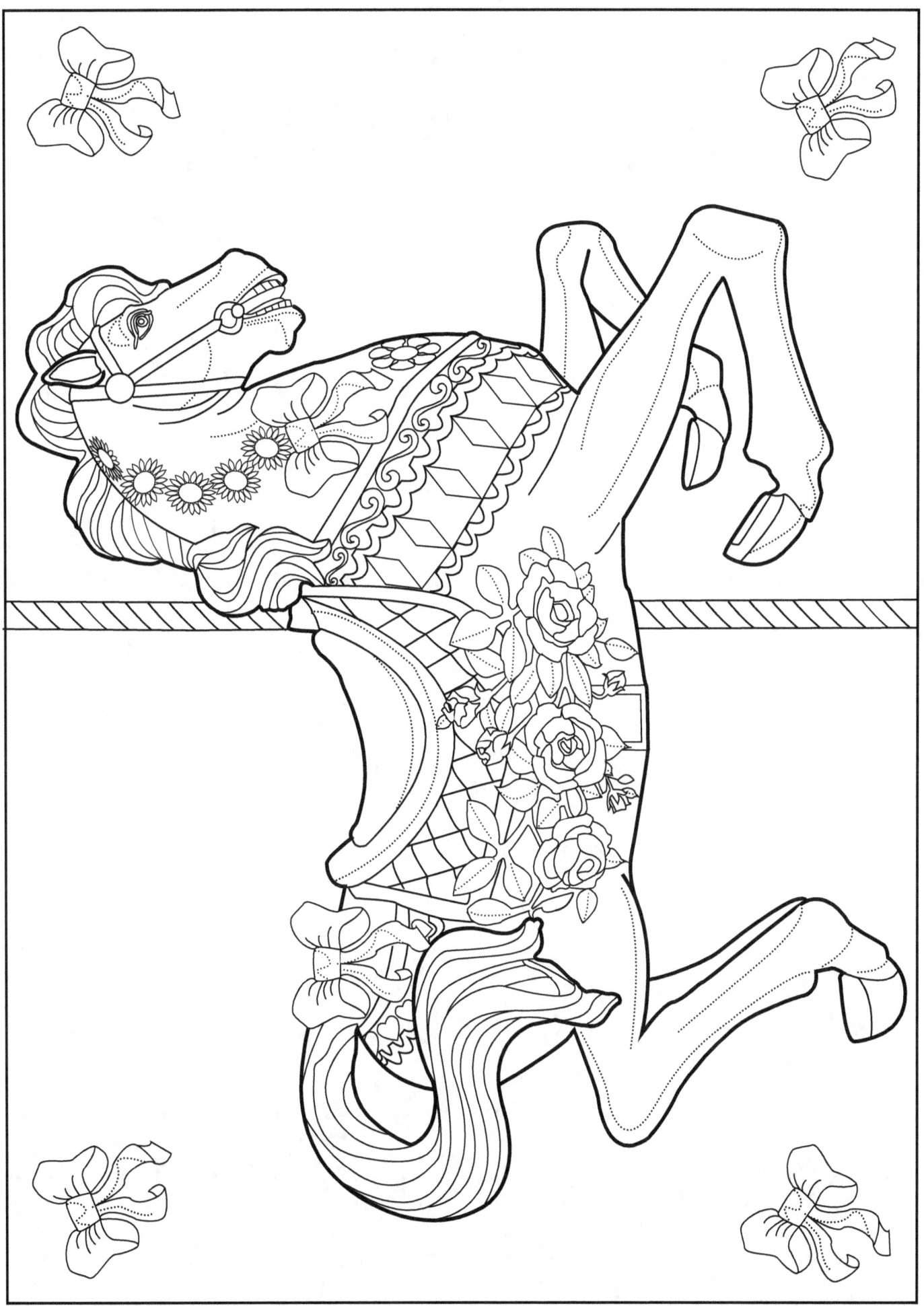

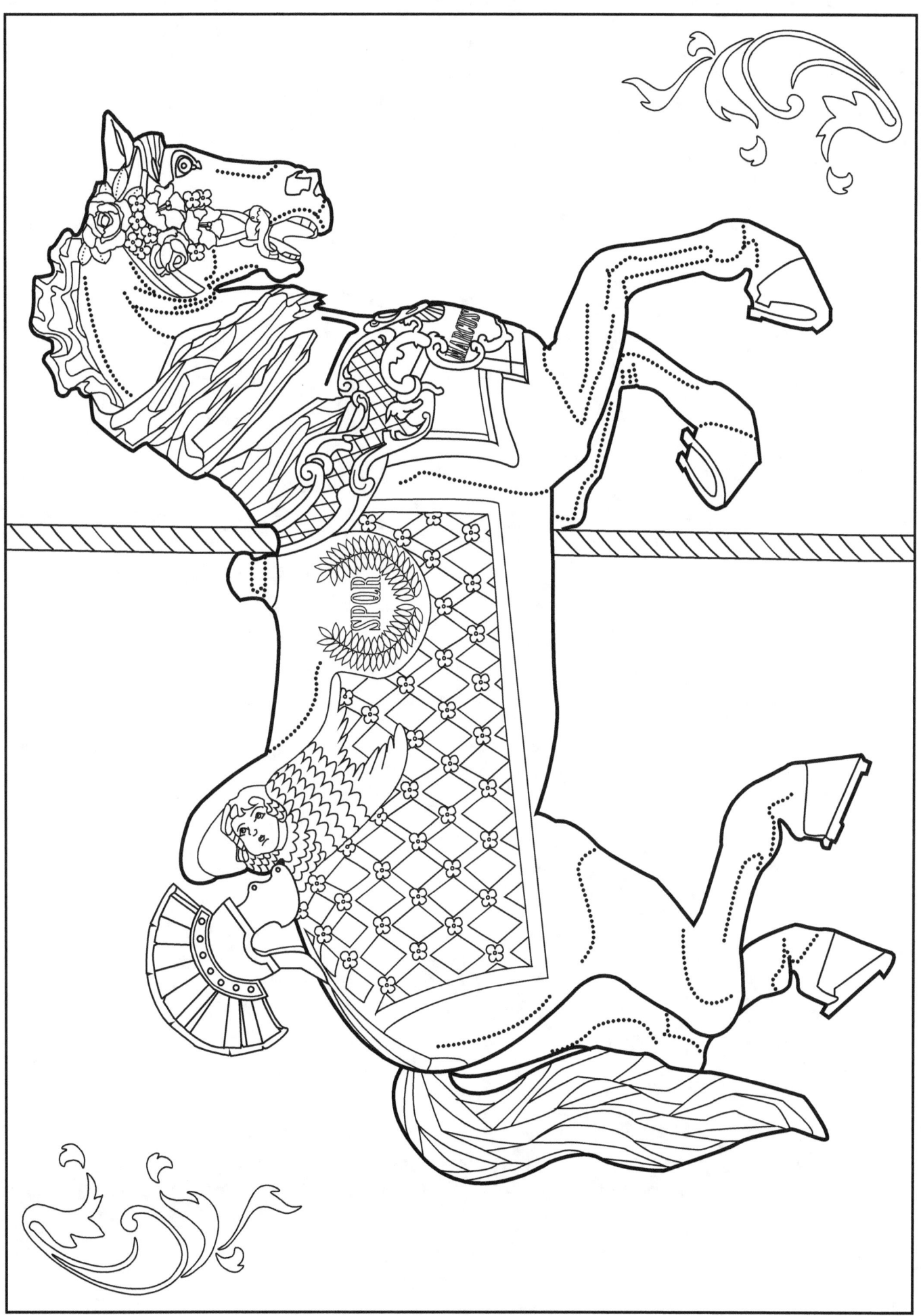

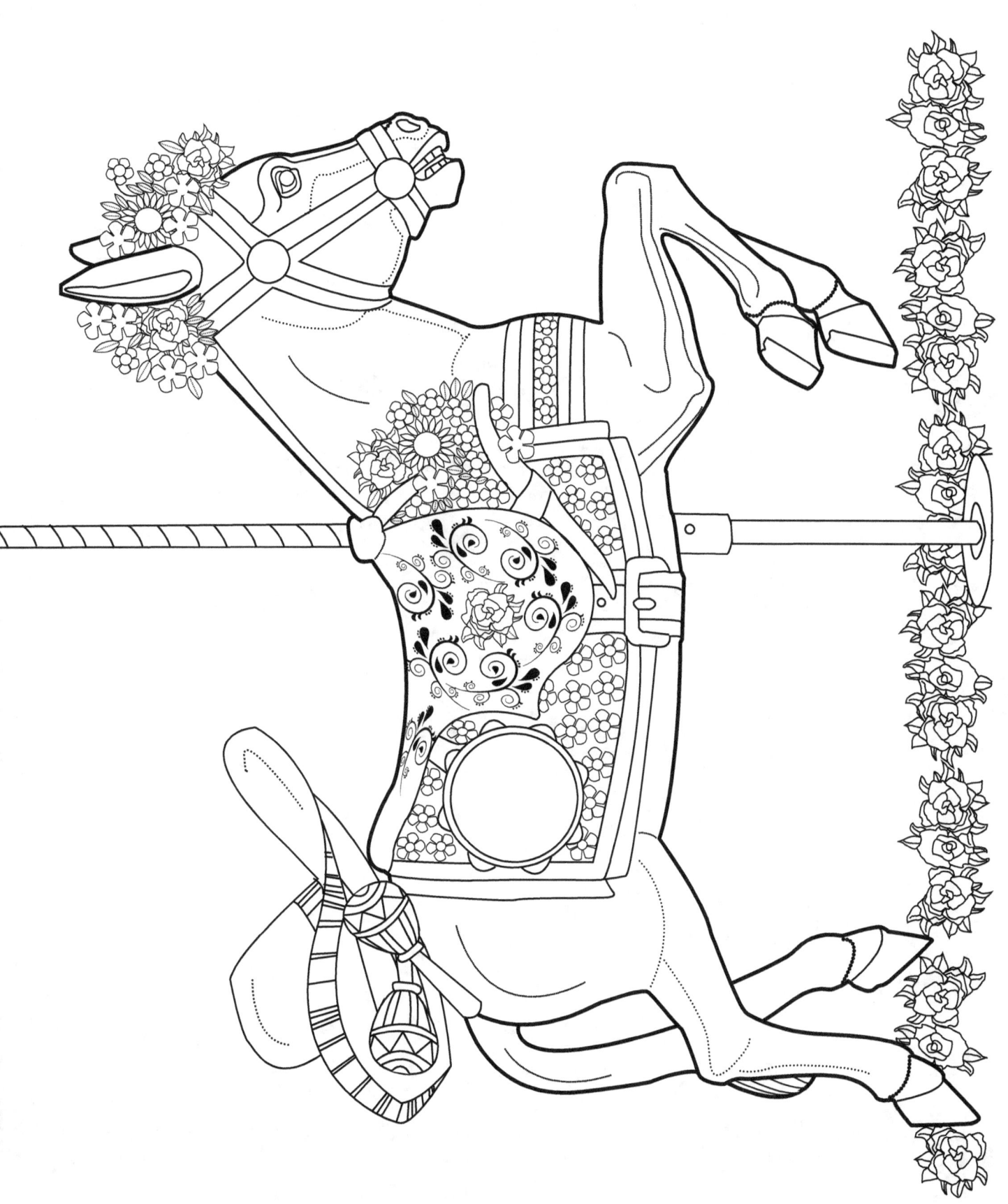

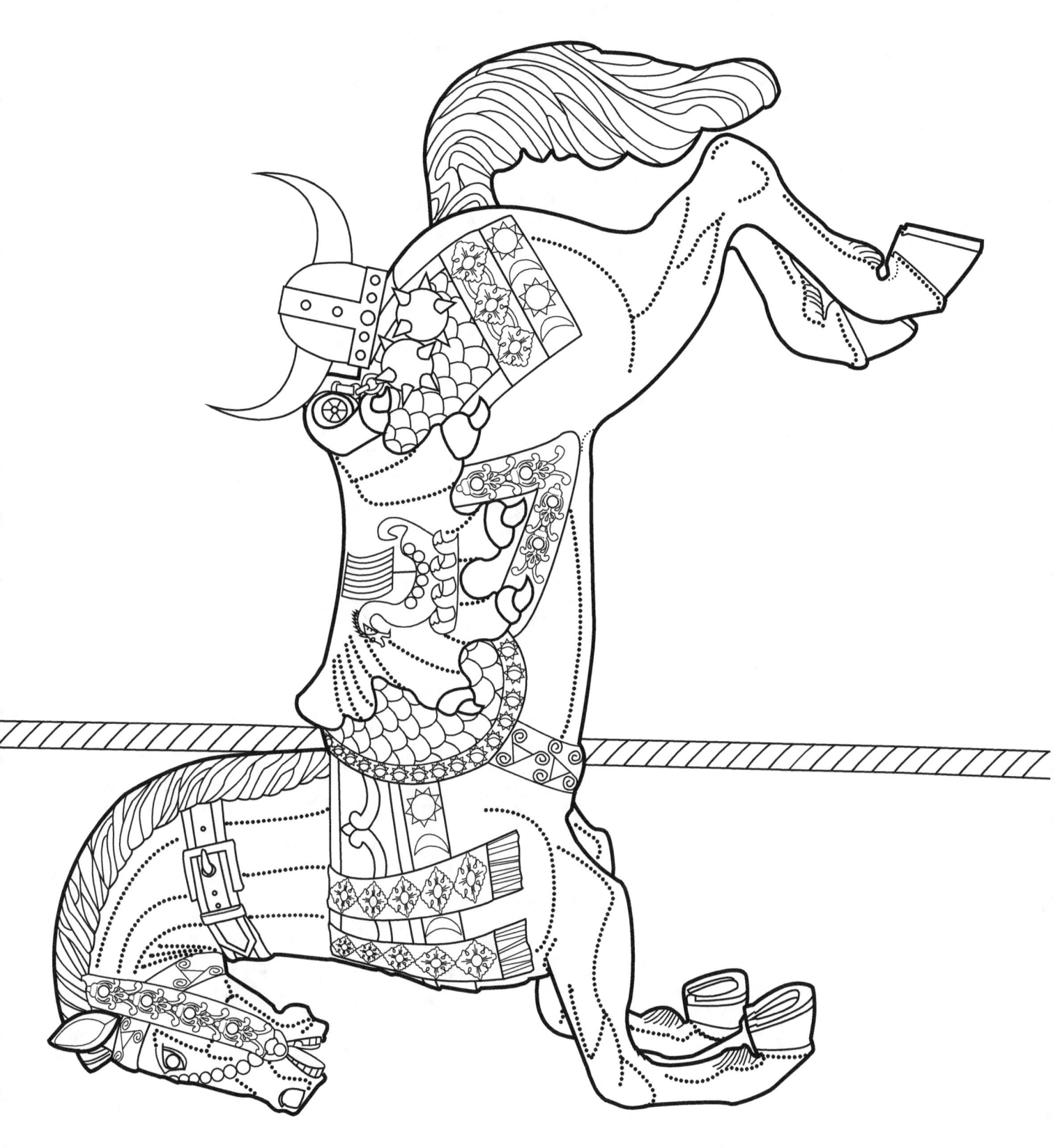

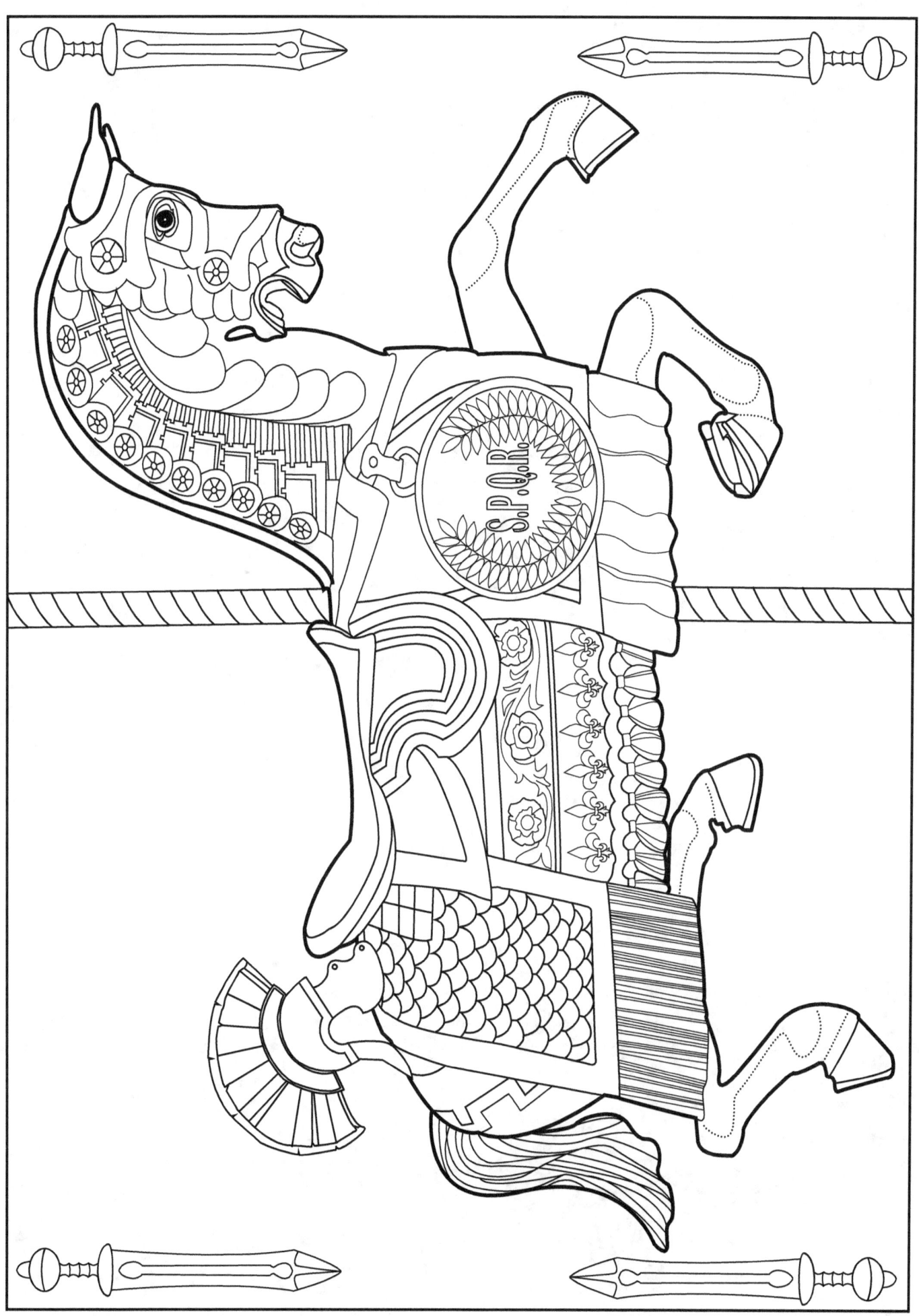

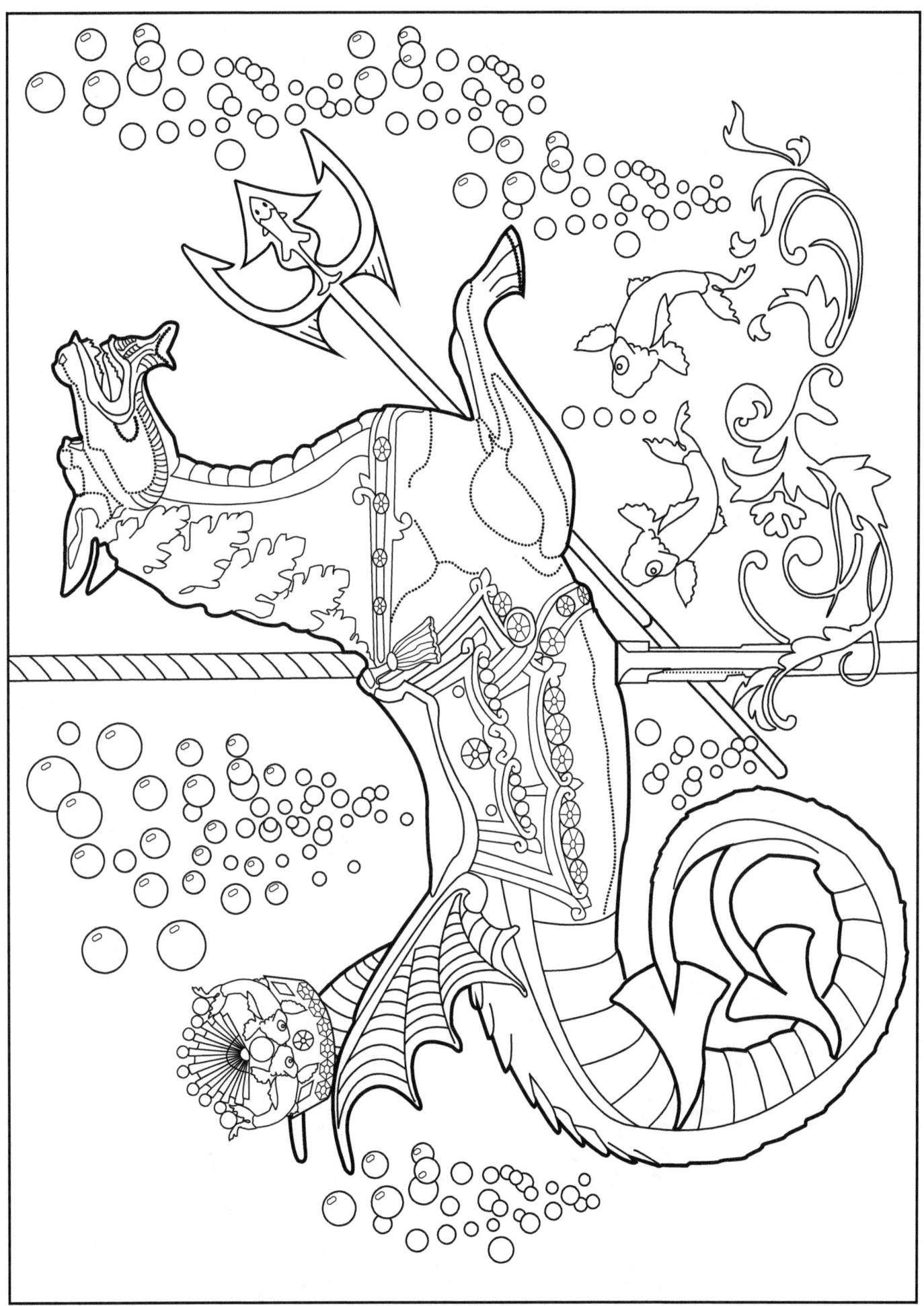

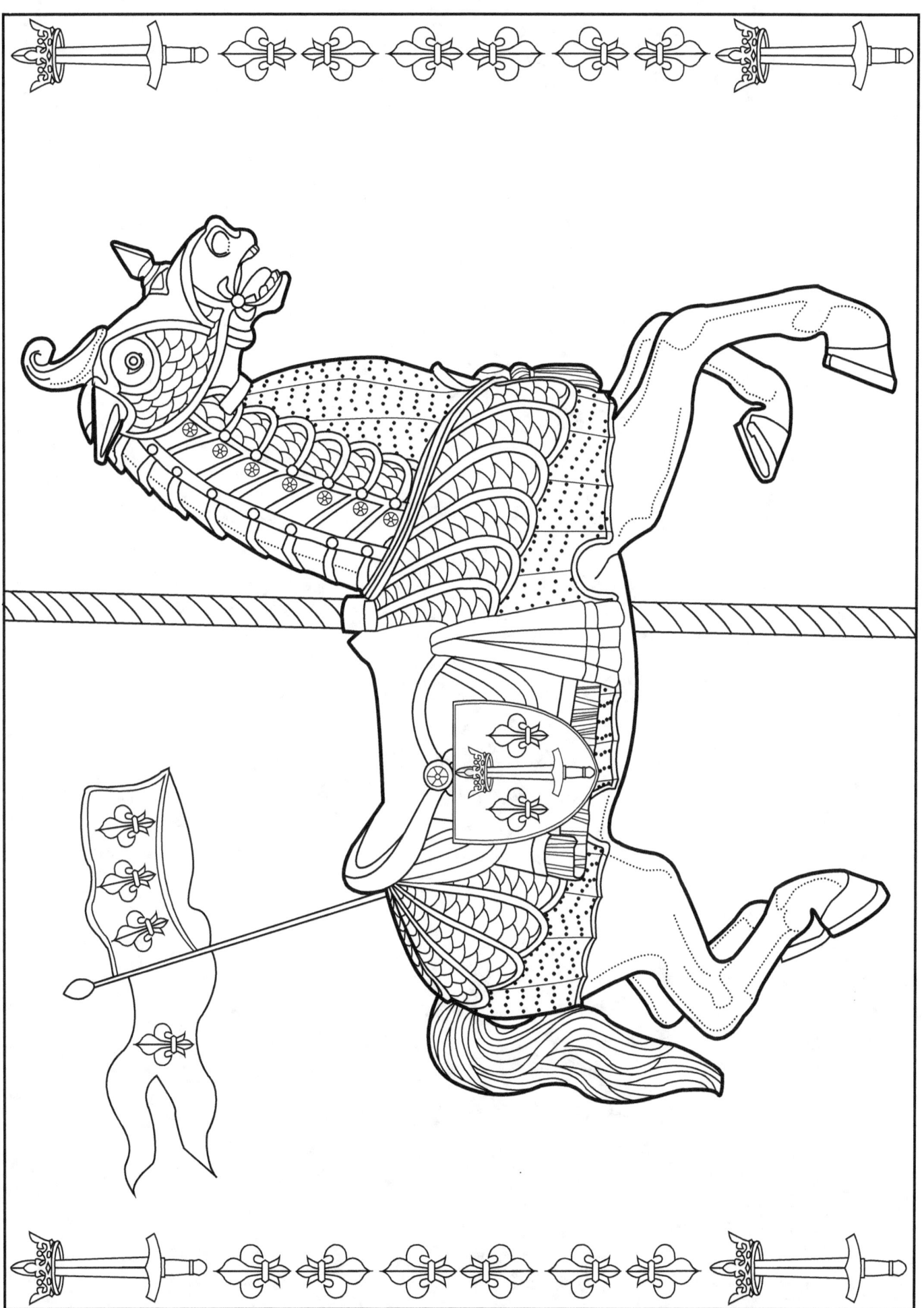

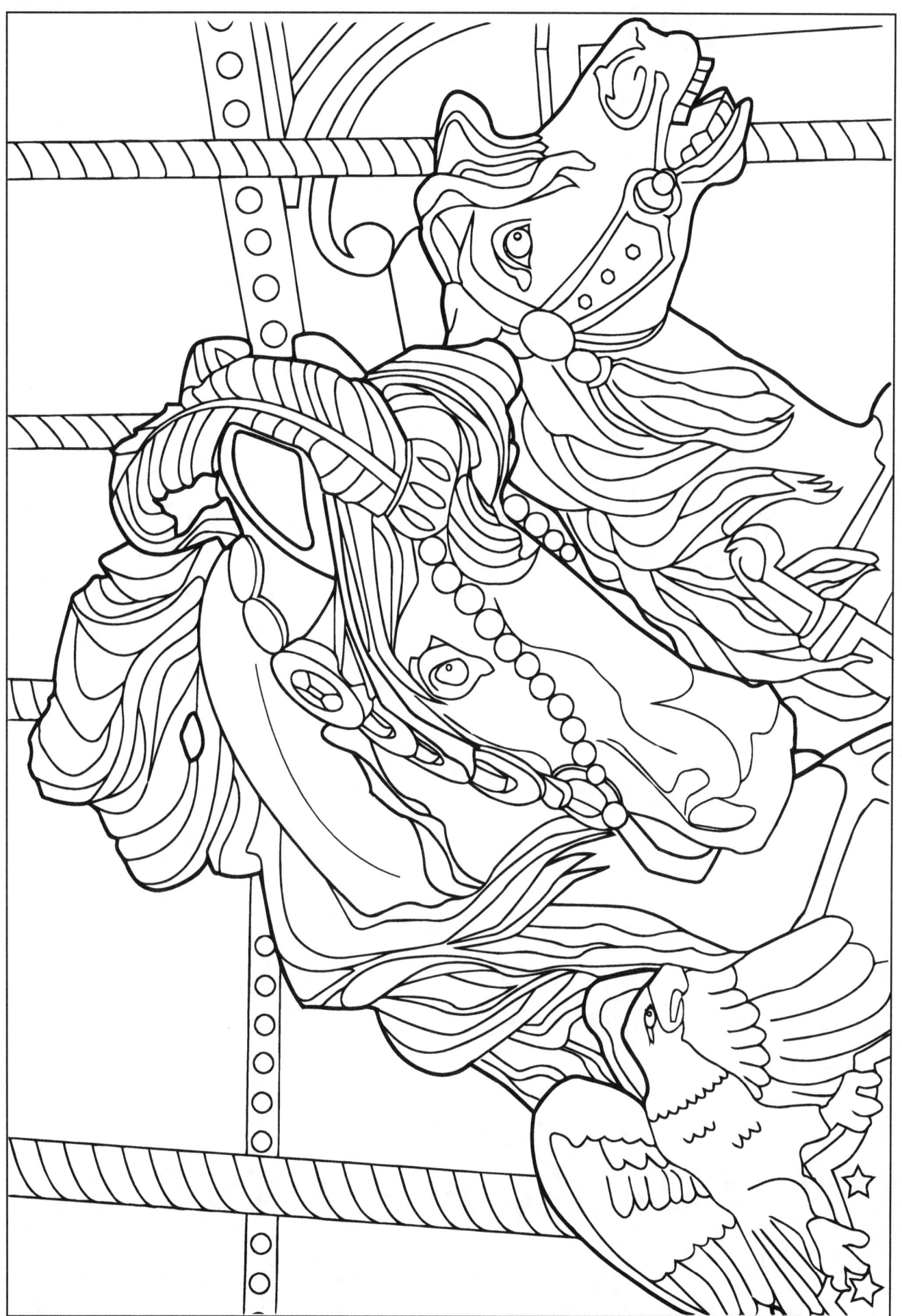

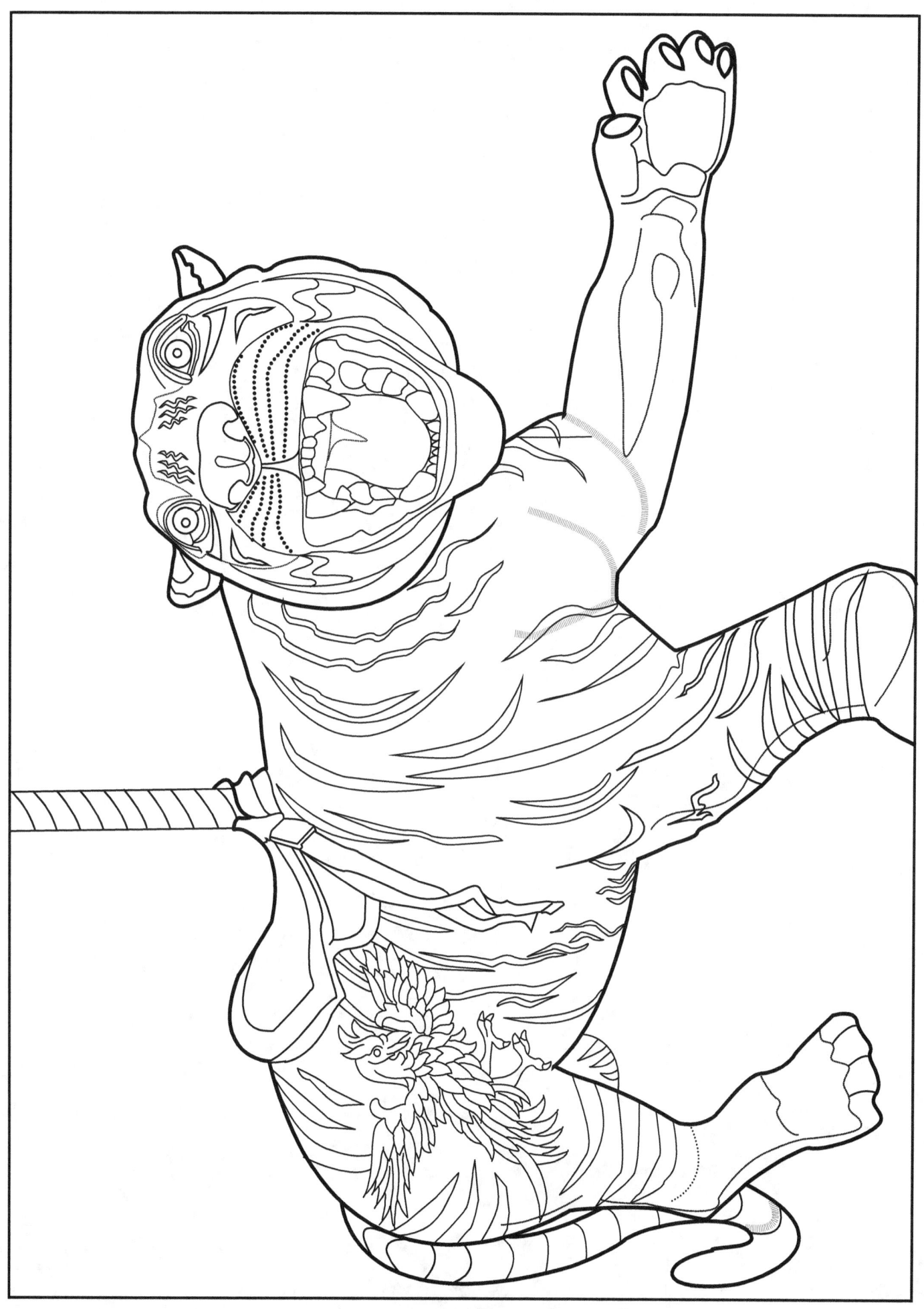

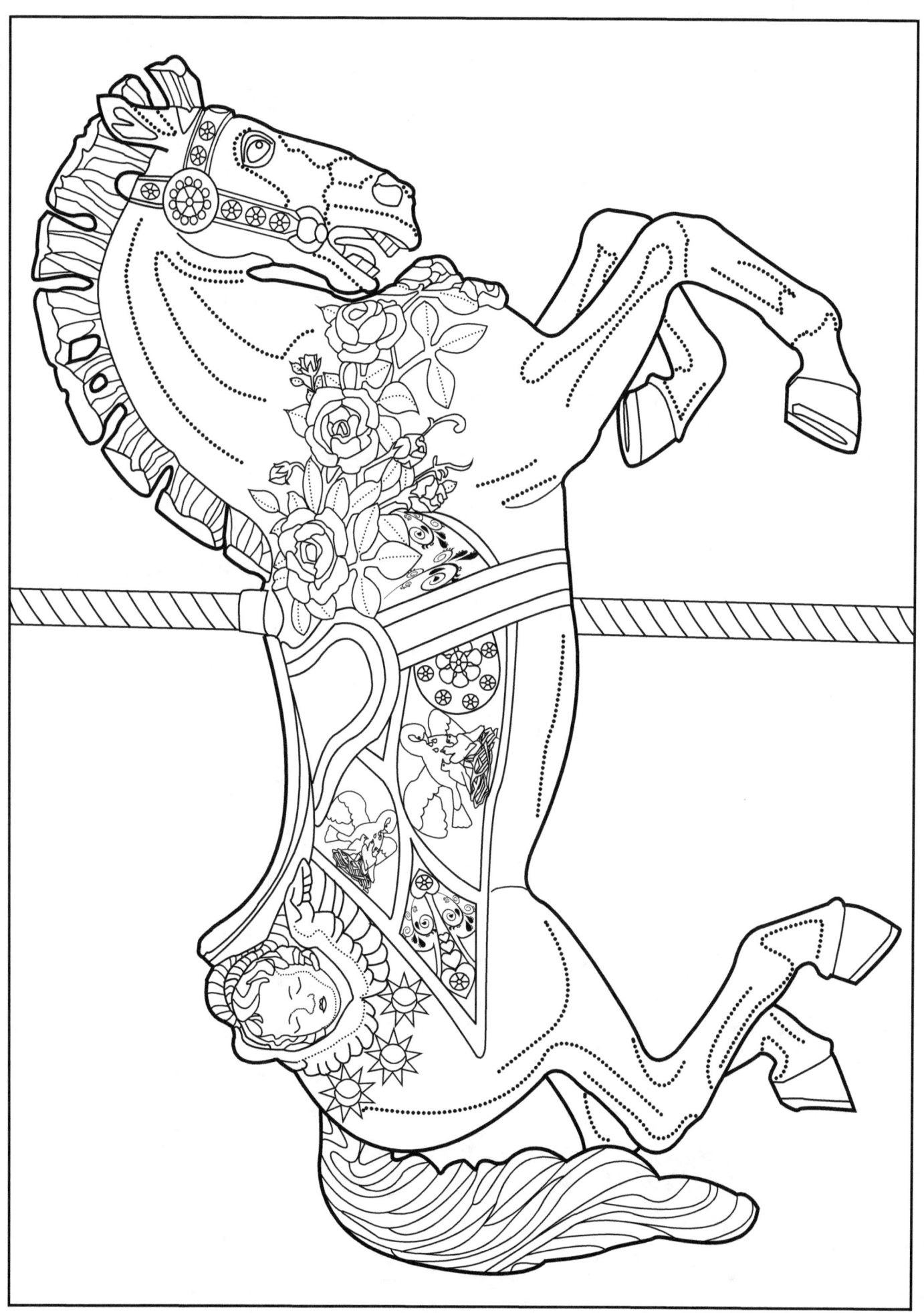

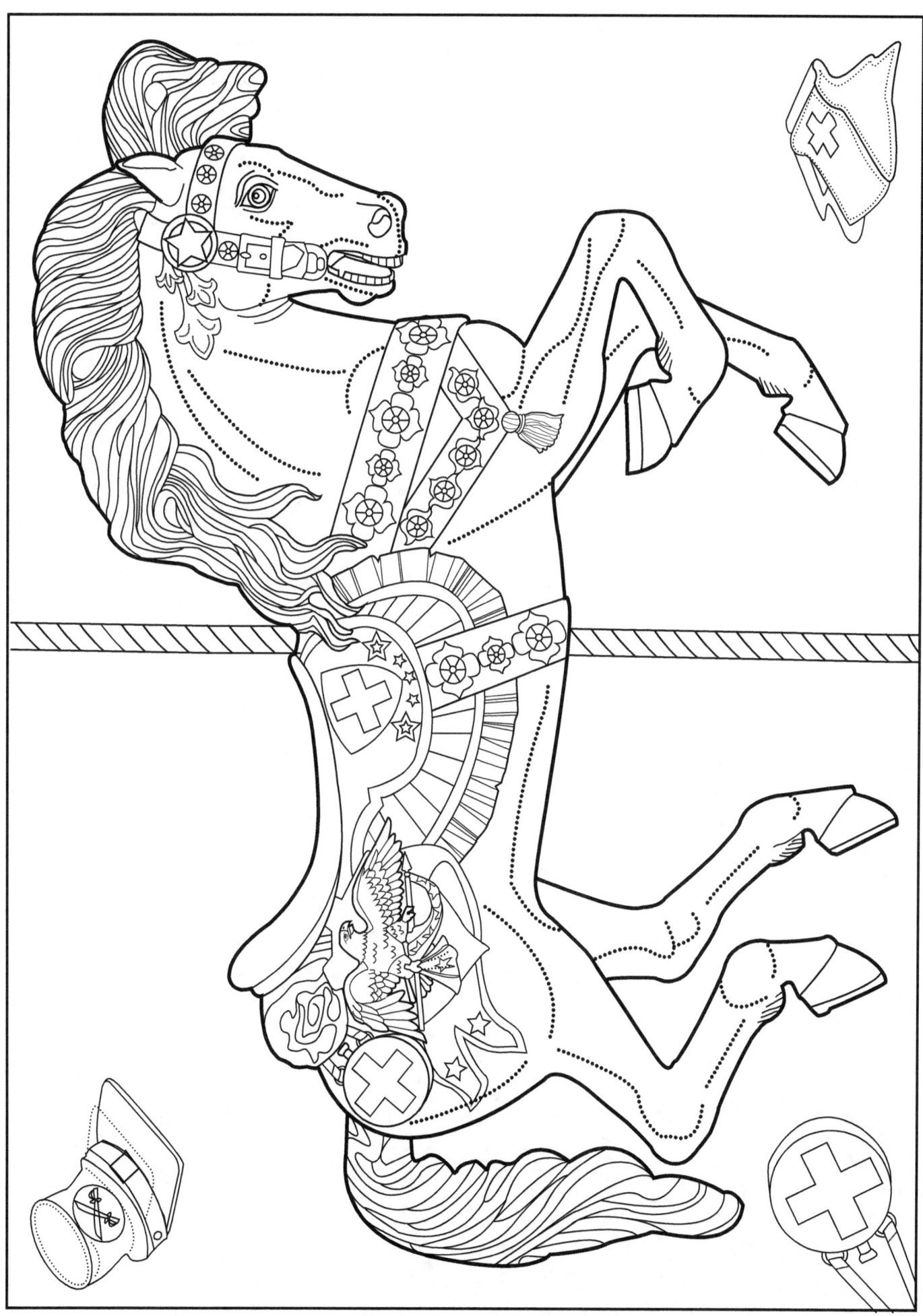

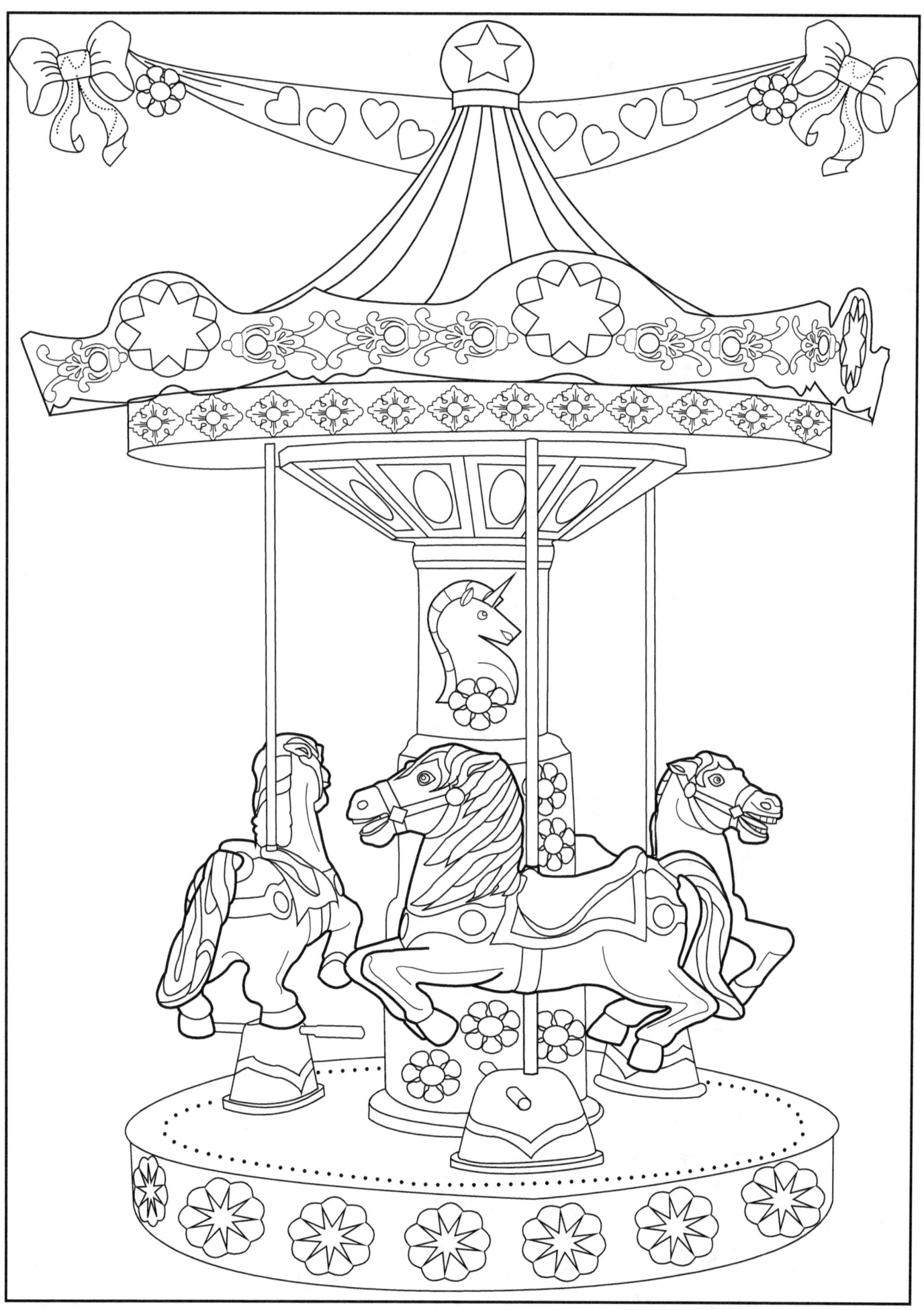

www.ingramcontent.com/pod-product-compliance
Lightning Source LLC
Chambersburg PA
CBHW081259180526
45170CB00007B/2494